THE STORY OF

MI VIDA

MY LIFE

AMALIA

WRITTEN BY
Amalia Garcia Kastberg

ILLUSTRATIONS BY
Gina Dell

Dedication

A Story about Amalia... By Amalia...

For Amalia, my namesake and beautiful, loving mother.

And to my wonderful dad, Pedro, who is no longer with us.

Thank you both for loving me unconditionally
and for giving me every opportunity in life.

To my big sister Gloria for always believing in me.
I couldn't ask for a better, more generous sister.

And to the person who loves me no matter what and is my rock — my husband, Orla.
You are beautiful inside and out. I can't imagine my life without you.

And to my two amazing sons, Sebastian and Vegas. You are my pride and joy.
You are such strong, caring young men. Please continue to make this
a better world for us all. You are our future.

And to all the immigrant children out there in the United States.
This is your home but never forget where you came from. It's what makes you special.

ISBN: 978-1-7355272-0-8

Published by Amalia Garcia Kastberg

Book design by Paintbox Creative
paintboxcreative.com

My name is Amalia.
Me llamo Amalia.

Hi. Hola. My name is Amalia.
Just like my mom.

Yes, I know it is a strange
and different name.

Everyone always points that out to me in the United States.

So much so that I was nicknamed Molly by my new American friends when I was little.

I was ok with it.
But wanted to spell it "Mali."
Like the African country and
truer to my real full name.

So this is my story.

It began in  Rio de Janeiro, Brazil.
I was born there in 1966.

My parents, Pedro and Amalia,
were working there at the time.
They were born and raised in Spain.

My dad always wanted to come to America. To pursue the "American Dream" and to give me and my sister a better life than the one he and my mom had growing up.

They grew up during the Spanish Civil War. It was a very tough time. They both had to stop going to school and start working to help support their families.

My dad came to the U.S. first with very little money in his pocket. He didn't know a word of English. He found a safe, affordable place to live in Washington D.C.'s Adams Morgan neighborhood.

When he had saved up enough money, my mom, sister and I left Brazil to join him.

The United States became our new home. I was about six months old.

Our apartment was more than
a place to live. It was home.
My parents worked very hard.
Day and night. But I never felt alone.
They loved me and my sister very much.

My parents wanted us to have a good, successful life in America.
But they also never wanted us to forget our Spanish way of life.
They created a "little Spain" for us in America.

We spoke Spanish at home. We ate yummy
Spanish food. We had Spanish friends.

I had the best of two worlds.
And at times, it was hard. I felt different.

My parents never learned to speak English.
They didn't have the time or money to go to school.

I learned English by watching TV, reading magazines and books, and
listening to other kids talk at the playground. I made American friends.
I enjoyed American food. I came to love the American way of life.

We didn't have a car for a long time,
so we walked everywhere.

To school. To the grocery.
To the park.

If something was too far away,
like our doctor, we took the bus.
We had a nice, simple life
filled with lots of love.

My dad worked at a bakery at night
so he could get his green card.
It was a big day when he got it!

Eventually, we all got green cards.
I was a "resident alien" as it was called.

I was happy to call the United States home.
But I still felt different. I was an "alien."

One day, I saw an American and a Spanish woman play in a Grand Slam tennis tournament.

"Which player do I want to win?" I asked myself.

And then I realized that it didn't matter.
I win either way.

The way I grew up and my life may be different.
But that's totally ok with me!

I am American and Spanish.
Soy Americana y Española.

My name is Amalia.
Me llamo Amalia.

CPSIA information can be obtained
at www.ICGtesting.com
Printed in the USA
LVHW070200051020
667927LV00015B/265